I WISH THAT I DIDN'T SOMETIMES, BUT...

...I REMEMBER EVERYTHING ABOUT THAT CURSED, UNSPEAKABLY UNHAPPY NIGHT TWELVE YEARS AGO...

MOM!!

DAD!!

TAKE THAT, YOU LITTLE NOTHING!

CRASH

FUME

I FLAME-BROIL MY MEAT...

...LIKE BURGER KING! AND BEELZE-BUB!!

CRACK

I HAVE TO TELL
YOU ONE LAST
THING ABOUT
THAT NIGHT.   I MUST GET IT
OUT.

EVEN THOUGH I WAS ONLY THREE
YEARS OLD, I AM ASHAMED THAT I DIDN'T
FIGHT THE PRAYER TO THE DEATH...

GRRRRR

YOU'RE VERY IMPRESSIVE AND SCARY, ORKNG—

MAY I CALL YOU ORKNG?

IS THAT YOUR LAST WISH?

OH, I HOPE NOT.

SAY, I'VE HEARD YOU HAVE LEVEL 4 STRENGTH.

TRUE OR FALSE?

WOW~!

THUD

AND YOU'RE A SHAPE-SHIFTER TOO?

THAT'S IT?

THAT'S ALL YOU CAN DO?

I CAME DOWN INTO THE SEWER FOR THAT?

THAT'S NOTHING, YOU LITTLE CHUMP.

NOW! WHEN HE'S CHANGING!

EXTERMINATED.

TWELVE YEARS HAVE PASSED SINCE THAT NIGHT.

I'M FIFTEEN NOW.

ALL GROWN UP. SORT OF.

SINCE MY MOM AND DAD DIED...

...SINCE I BECAME AN ALIEN HUNTER...

...I'VE BEEN KIDNAPPED BY FACELESS METALLIC HUMANOIDS.

TWICE.

I'VE BEEN CHASED AND CAPTURED BY A SHAPE-SHIFTING PROTO-PLASM IN LONDON WHO WANTED TO MAKE ME INTO A JELLY SANDWICH, WITHOUT THE BREAD.

I'VE BEEN IN HAND-TO-ANTENNAE COMBAT WITH AN ENTIRE CIVILIZATION OF INSECTS IN MEXICO CITY, CUERNAVACA, AND ACAPULCO.

I'VE HAD MY FACE RUN OVER AGAIN AND AGAIN—FOR DAYS—BY SELF-REPLICATING MACHINES THAT WERE ABOUT TO TAKE OVER DETROIT.

A BILLION OR SO "LITTLE WAILING MOUTHS" CONNECTED THROUGH AN ELECTRICAL NETWORK TO A SINGLE MIND ATE AND DIGESTED ME IN HAMBURG, GERMANY.

THEY WERE ALL ON THIS LIST, AND NOW THEY'RE ALL GONE.

LET ME CHECK.

THE LIST—

IT CONTAINS THE NAMES, FULL DESCRIPTIONS...

...AND APPROXIMATE WHEREABOUTS OF THE KNOWN OUTLAW ALIENS CURRENTLY ROAMING THE EARTH.

AND TRUST ME ON THIS—

THEY ARE OUT THERE, WATCHING AND STUDYING US.

CREAK

COOL,
LOOKS LIKE
NO ONE
BROKE IN.

WHO'S
NEXT...?

NUMBER 6: ERGENT SETH.

HE'S BASED IN L.A., SOMEWHERE CALLED MALIBU.

HE SPECIALIZES IN GENOCIDE, AND HE'S ALREADY DEVASTATED ALPAR NOK.

NOW HE'S AFTER TERRA FIRMA — EARTH — TO DESTROY EVERY LIFE-FORM.

IT'S CRUCIAL TO STOP HIM BEFORE HE GETS ON A ROLL...

...SO THE LIST STRONGLY RECOMMENDS HIM AS THE NEXT TARGET.

DING DONG..

L.A....

TIME TO LEAVE THIS HOUSE.

HUH?

I NEVER HAVE VISITORS. WHO CAN IT BE?

HE WENT TO HIGH SCHOOL WHEN HE WAS TEN.

HE HAS AN IQ, OH, SOME-WHERE IN THE 190s.

HE GRADUATED FROM M.I.T. LAST YEAR. OUR DANNY HAS A DEGREE IN MOLECULAR ENGINEERING.

WE'RE VERY PROUD OF HIM.

IS THAT SO?

IN THAT CASE, IF YOU WOULD JUST GO GET HIS DIPLOMA...

...COLLEGE OR HIGH SCHOOL WOULD BE FINE.

YOU'LL SEE HIS DIPLOMA WHEN WE SEE A WARRANT.

NOW YOU AND SILENT BOB THERE CAN LEAVE.

WOULDN'T WANT YOU TO CATCH THE MEASLES.

IT'LL ACTUALLY BE FUN HAULING YOU, YOUR WIFE, AND YOUR "GENIUS" SON IN WHEN WE COME BACK WITH THAT WARRANT.

OF COURSE, TECHNICALLY THEY'RE NOT MY PARENTS. MY REAL PARENTS ARE DEAD.

I DON'T THINK HE WAS KIDDING.

BROOM

PORTLAND POLICE

MY IMAGINED PARENTS ARE PROBABLY JUST MENTAL PROJECTIONS THAT I MAKE REAL.

I KNOW, DAD.

I'LL BE OUT OF HERE BEFORE THEY GET TO THE END OF OUR STREET.

I'M GOING AFTER NUMBER 6 NEXT.

ERGENT SETH.

I HAVE THESE POWERS.

I CAN CREATE THINGS, SORT OF.

OH, DANIEL, ARE YOU SURE ABOUT THAT?

NUMBER 6 MIGHT BE WAY TOO MUCH, WAY TOO SOON.

DON'T WORRY, MOM.

SAY, SOMETHING AS SIMPLE AS A SIGN LIKE THIS?

LA

HOONK

VROOM

MY MOM AND DAD AND FRIENDS ARE EASY TOO.

I CREATE THEM A LOT, WHEN I'M AFRAID OR LONELY.

THEY'RE LIKE A RECIPE YOU'VE DONE OVER AND OVER AGAIN UNTIL YOU CAN DO IT IN YOUR SLEEP.

GAH!

WHO SENT YOU AFTER ME?!

I WANT TO KNOW RIGHT NOW!!

HEHEHEHEHE HEH

URK!

SO—

NUMBER 6 SOMEHOW KNOWS I'M COMING.

WHAT OTHER POWERS DOES ERGENT SETH HAVE THAT ARE AS IMPRESSIVE AS MY OWN?

COLD.

ONLY
NATURAL,
I GUESS.

WISH I HAD A HOT MEAL.

MAYBE I SHOULD HEAT UP THE GATORADE OVER THE FIRE...

!!

......

...COME TO THINK OF IT...

...SOME OF THE ALIEN OUTLAWS CAN SEE IN THE DARK LIKE IT'S DAYLIGHT.

WHAT IF ONE OF THEM'S LURKING OUT HERE...?!

WHY DID I STAY UP LATE WATCHING THE BLAIR WITCH PROJECT A FEW NIGHTS AGO?!

MAYBE I SHOULD HAVE TRIED HARDER TO FIND A TOWN.

I DON'T WANNA BE ALONE—!!

RUSTLE

THERE YOU ARE.

DANIEL X

CHAPTER 2

HEY, WILLY.

SURVIVAL TRAINING.

I LOVE IT.

THE GREAT OUTDOORS!

THE PACIFIC NORTHWEST! WOW!

WILLY IS AROUND MY AGE—FIFTEEN OR SO.

HE'S ALWAYS READY, WILLING, AND ABLE TO TRY ANYTHING, AND MIX IT UP WITH ANY *THING*.

YOU KNOW HOW TO TRAVEL, DANIEL.

IF ANYONE ENJOYS CHASING DOWN ALIENS AS MUCH AS I DO, IT'S WILLY.

CHEX MIX!

RIGHT-EOUS!

JOE-JOE, ON THE OTHER HAND...

...IS MORE LIKE ALL STOMACH.

HEY! THAT WAS SUPPOSED TO BE MY BREAKFAST TOMORROW!

NO WONDER IT WAS SO GOOD!

WHICH IS CRAZY, BECAUSE HE'S SUPER SKINNY.

HE'S ALSO MESSY, AN ATHLETE AT NOTHING BUT COMPETITIVE EATING, AND THE MOST SARCASTIC, FUNNIEST MOTORMOUTH I KNOW.

OH, WOW!

SPRUCE, CEDARS...

...DOUGLAS FIRS, CYPRESSES.

AMAZING!

I LOVE IT HERE.

GREAT SPOT, DANIEL.

SHE'S TALL, WITH PIN-STRAIGHT BLOND HAIR THAT FLOWS LIKE A WATERFALL OF FLAME DOWN HER BACK.

SHE'S PROBABLY THE MOST BEAUTIFUL GIRL I'VE EVER SEEN—JUST MY OPINION, OF COURSE.

BUT THE NEAT PART IS THAT, HANDS DOWN, DANA'S THE MOST GENUINE PERSON I'VE MET.

NO EGO, NO BIG HEAD, NO AGENDA.

SWEET SPOT, DANIEL.

I LOVE THE COLD BY ITSELF, BUT *WET* TOO? AND LOUSY GRUB.

JOE'S ACTUALLY RIGHT FOR ONCE. THIS PLACE IS A DUMP.

A DUMP?!

THE PACIFIC NORTHWEST IS LIKE ONE OF THE BIOLOGICALLY RICHEST AREAS IN NORTH AMERICA.

MAYBE IN ALL THE TEMPERATE AREAS OF THE WORLD.

BESIDES ALL OF THE CONIFEROUS GROWTH...

...IT'S HOME TO THE MOURNING DOVE AND THE WESTERN FENCE LIZARD.

HEY, YOU'RE RIGHT, EMMA.

THIS ECO-BIOSYSTEM THINGY IS REALLY STARTING TO GROW ON ME. IN FACT...

WILL YOU MARRY ME?

SERI-OUSLY. I LOVE YOU, TREE.

HEY!!

ENOUGH, CLOWN BOY.

I CALL TRIVIAL PURSUIT.

46

FIRST QUESTION, DANA.

CATEGORY IS ENTERTAINMENT. WHO PLAYED THE ROLE OF GEORGE BAILEY IN FRANK CAPRA'S CHRISTMAS CLASSIC, *IT'S A WONDERFUL LIFE*?

I KNOW YOU KNOW IT, GIRL.

SAMUEL L. JACKSON...

...

JIMMY STEWART.

NO, WAIT. IT WAS MINI-ME!

YOU GO, GIRL.

NEXT QUESTION — JOE.

CATEGORY IS THEORETICAL PHYSICS.

WHAT?!

IN QUANTUM ELECTRODYNAMICS, WHAT IS THE FULL SCATTERING AMPLITUDE THE SUM OF?

WH-WH-WHAT?!

THEORETICAL PHYSICS! E=MC². HOW SHOULD I KNOW? LET ME SEE THAT CARD!

INCOR-RECT.

SCIENCE AND NATURE.

DANIEL, YOUR TURN.

WHAT DOES ELEPHANT MEAN IN LATIN?

AN ELEPHANT QUES-TION!

I GET THE THERMO WHATZIT AND DANIEL, THE ELEPHANT NERD, GETS AN ELE-PHANT QUESTION?

BESIDES, HE KNOWS LATIN.

AND ABOUT A HUNDRED OTHER LAN-GUAGES.

HUGE ARCH.

ELE MEANS ARCH AND PHANT MEANS HUGE.

CORRECT.

TCH!

YOU KNOW WHAT, GUYS? I THINK I'M GONNA HIT THE SACK.

I'VE HAD A LONG, HARD ONE TODAY.

YOU DO LOOK TIRED, SO GET SOME REST.

YOU GOT MY BACK TONIGHT?

ANYTHING GETS CLOSE TO THIS CAMPFIRE THAT JOE CAN'T EAT...

...YOU'RE GOING TO BE THE FIRST TO KNOW.

HEY, YOU. WHY ARE YOU STILL UP?

YOU SHOULD GET SOME REST.

WELL...

...WHY DO I ONLY GET TO MEET THE BAD ALIENS?

I'M PRETTY SURE THERE ARE SOME GOOD ONES OUT THERE, BUT I'VE NEVER MET ONE.

DO YOU THINK I'LL EVER GET TO MEET A GOOD ALIEN?

YOU MEET ONE EVERY DAY.

EVERY TIME YOU LOOK IN A MIRROR.

YOU MEAN ME?

YOU THINK I'M AN ALIEN TOO?

IT WOULDN'T MAKE ANY SENSE IF YOU'RE NOT.

ANYWAY, DON'T GET TOO DEEP INTO THOSE THOUGHTS AND GO TO SLEEP.

GOOD NIGHT, DANNYBOY.

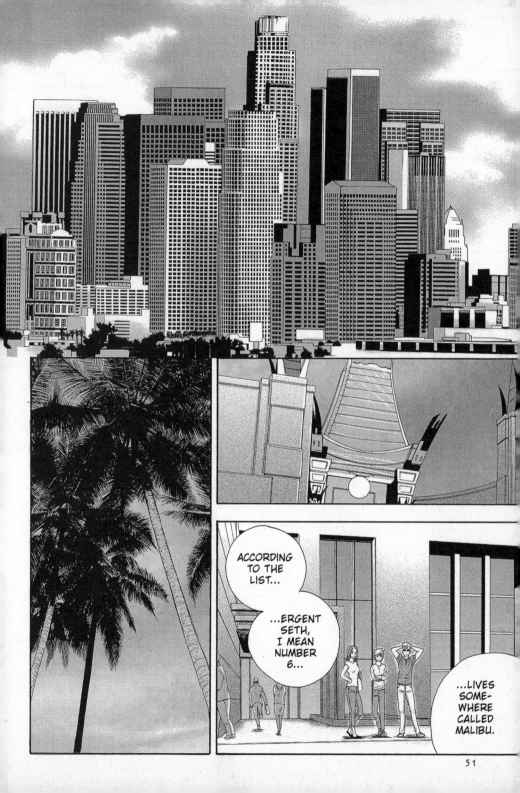

ACCORDING TO THE LIST...

...ERGENT SETH, I MEAN NUMBER 6...

...LIVES SOME-WHERE CALLED MALIBU.

WE'LL BE GOING NOW...

I'M GLAD WE GOT A PLACE YOU LIKE.

NO, WAIT!

STAY AROUND FOR DINNER. I'LL COOK!

I SHOULD TRY OUT THIS GOURMET KITCHEN, RIGHT?

GLENDALE HIGH SCHOOL

I WANT TO TRY TO BLEND INTO THE COMMUNITY...

...AND ESPECIALLY AVOID A TRUANT SQUAD RUN-IN LIKE THE ONE IN PORTLAND.

SO I DECIDED I'D BETTER AT LEAST SIGN UP FOR SCHOOL. BUT...

THIS IS BORING!!

HA...SO THIS IS HIGH SCHOOL.

MURMUR MURMUR

UGH.

MY SNEAKERS ARE SO SIX MONTHS AGO.

EVERY-BODY'S LOOKING AT ME! DON'T LOOK AT ME. PLEASE!

EVERY-BODY'S CHECKING OUT MY SHOES.

...

WELL, WELL. AMANDA'S DEFINITELY FLIRTING WITH ME.

I HATE THIS...

FIRST DAY'S OVER, AND I HAVEN'T EVEN TALKED TO ANYBODY.

I DON'T WANT TO DO THIS ANYMORE. I HATE THIS SCHOOL.

WHOSE THOUGHTS ARE THESE?

WOW...

HI.

SORRY TO BOTHER YOU. UMM...

...COULD YOU TELL ME WHERE THE LIBRARY IS?

NO IDEA.

I'M NEW HERE.

SO AM I.

SAY, COULD I GIVE YOU A HAND WITH THOSE BOOKS?

I'M DANIEL.

NOT THAT YOU ASKED.

SO DO YOU HAVE A LAST NAME TOO, DANIEL?

ERM, HOPPER. DANIEL HOPPER.

GORGEOUS —!!

I'M PHOEBE COOK.

NICE TO MEET YOU, DANIEL HOPPER.

I ACTUALLY COULD USE SOME HELP. JUST TO GET MY LOCKER BACK OPEN.

THUD

FRANKLY, I DON'T KNOW IF I CAN LUG ALL THESE BOOKS HOME.

YOU'RE IN LUCK. LUGGING IS ONE OF MY BETTER TALENTS.

I THOUGHT YOU WERE LOOKING FOR THE LIBRARY, DANIEL.

I GOT A BETTER OFFER, I GUESS.

I GUESS YOU DID.

WELL, LET'S SEE HOW YOU LUG.

WOW, YOU DO MOVE AROUND A LOT.

TOO MUCH.

MY FAMILY MOVES A LOT TOO.

THEY'RE KIND OF FREE SPIRITS.

DANIEL IS GORGEOUS!

I WONDER IF HE WOULD MAYBE ASK ME OUT?

...!!

IT'S OKAY, DANIEL.

GO FOR IT.

SO THIS IS IT. THAT'S MY PLACE.

EH-HEH-HEH.

AH-HA-HA.

WHY DON'T WE GO TO A MOVIE, OR MAYBE EXPLORE GLENDALE SOMETIME?

OKAY.

THE MOVIES, WHATEVER. THAT'D BE GREAT. GOOD.

YOU KNOW WHAT I MEAN.

BYE-BYE.

WERE YOU REALLY LOOKING FOR THE LIBRARY?

NOPE.

I WAS LOOKING FOR YOU.

GOOD ANSWER.

AND NO, I DIDN'T CREATE PHOEBE COOK, IN CASE YOU'RE ONE OF THOSE PEOPLE WHO LIKE TO LOOK AHEAD IN A STORY.

AAAAH~

AAAAH~

BOLT

NOTHING BETTER TO GET YOUR MIND OFF GIRLS THAN THINKING ABOUT ALIENS.

BEEP

ALIEN: ERGENT SETH, NUMBER 6
HUMAN ALIAS(ES): ? CHANGES NAMES ON AN AS-NEEDED BASIS, OFTEN HOURLY.
AREA OF INFESTATION: L.A. AND ORANGE COUNTY, CALIFORNIA, CENTRAL CITY, EAST L.A. ARIZONA, NEVADA, MEXICO, SOUTH AND CENTRAL AMERICA, AND STILL BRANCHING OUT.
ILLEGAL ACTIVITIES: DRUG DEALING, MASS MURDER, ABDUCTIONS, TORTURE, MIND CONTROL, AND POSSESSION. DID WE MENTION MASS MURDER?

PLANET OF ORIGIN: GORTO 4.
ALIEN SPECIES: VERMGYPIAN (SEE FOOTNOTE).
CURRENT DANGER LEVEL: EXTREMELY HIGH. SETH'S GOAL IS TO DE-POPULATE EARTH, THEN COLONIZE IT WITH HIS SPECIES. THIS VIOLATES EVERY MORAL AND ETHICAL CODE EXTANT.
SPECIAL ABILITIES: TELEPATHY, EXTRATERRESTRIAL LEVEL 7 SPEED, LEVEL 7 STRENGTH, SHAPE-SHIFTING, CUNNING, GENERAL VICIOUSNESS.

SO THIS IS WHERE NUM- BER 6 DOES HIS NASTIEST SCUT WORK.

THIS PART OF L.A. SEEMS LIKE A WAR ZONE WITH PALM TREES.

IT SEEMS QUIET TODAY, THOUGH.

FWSH

FWSH

!!

WHAT THE HELL IS—?!

AAAAACK!!

MICHELLE!!

HAS ANYONE SEEN MY DAUGHTER?!

SHE'S NINE WITH BROWN HAIR AND—

SHE JUST DISAPPEARED!!

MY SON!!

MY SON DISAPPEARED TOO!

WHAT'S GOING ON?!

MY BABY!!

!!

THAT SHOULD DO FOR TODAY.

YES, SIR.

RETREAT.

THUD

!

FWSH

TSK. I WAS TOO LATE.

PHOE-
BE.

THERE
YOU
ARE.

SHE
LOOKS A
BIT BLUE
TODAY...

I'VE BEEN
LOOKING
EVERY-
WHERE
FOR YOU,
DANIEL.

I'VE BEEN LOOKING EVERYWHERE FOR YOU DANIEL♡

SORRY,
DANA.

SO, YOU
HEARD
THE
NEWS?

ABOUT
THE
KIDS...

AH. SHE
DEFENITELY
SEEMS
UPSET.

MAYBE I SHOULD TALK ABOUT SOMETHING ELSE.

HOW ABOUT THAT MOVIE?

MAYBE FRIDAY?

AM I BEING TOO PUSHY?

THIS FRIDAY? YES!

NO, WAIT.

MAYBE I SHOULDN'T SEEM TOO EAGER. HE MIGHT GET THE WRONG IDEA.

...

UM.

CAN I LET YOU KNOW? I MIGHT HAVE TO BABYSIT AT HOME.

SURE. NO WORRIES.

AH, LOOK.

THAT'S MY HOUSE.

AWWW! HOW CUTE!

WHAT'S YOUR CAT'S NAME?

MY CAT?

DANIEL X

CHAPTER 3

THEY DID A GREAT JOB MAKING A MESS.

...OR DIE!

WHA—?!

ALL DONE.

OH, ALREADY?

THAT WAS QUICK.

SERIOUSLY, GUYS...

...I'M NOTHING WITHOUT YOU.

AND YOU THANK US HOW...?

I WAS GONNA ORDER PIZZ—

PIZZA! I'LL ORDER!!

W-W-W-WAIT!! I CAN'T LET YOU ORDE—

NO, NOT ONE WITH EVERYTHING.

ONE OF EVERYTHING. I'D LIKE THE ENTIRE MENU.

SHHH.

HELLO?

IN FACT, MAKE IT TWO ENTIRE MENUS.

DOMINO'S?

RING

I DON'T DO PROCESSED FLOUR. HELLO? THIS IS CALIFORNIA.

THERE HAS TO BE A WHOLE FOODS AROUND HERE.

HUH?

IT SHOULD BE THE PIZZA PLACE, CONFIRMING JOE'S INSANE ORDER.

RING

GIMME.

DON'T CANCEL ANYTHING!

HELLO?

HELLO, INDEED.

!!! IT'S SETH!

...WHO'S THIS?

WHO'S THIS? NOW IS THAT REMOTELY PROPER ETIQUETTE?

WOULDN'T "MAY I HELP YOU?" BE A TAD MORE POLITE? BAD ENOUGH THEY SEND A BOY FOR ME, BUT A CRUDE AMERICAN ONE WITH NO MANNERS?

NONETHE-LESS, TO ANSWER YOUR IMPOLITE QUESTION, I THINK YOU KNOW WHO I AM.

THOUGH I DARE-SAY, IF YOU DON'T FOLLOW MY ADVICE VERY, VERY SOON...

NOTHING THAT HAS EVER ENCOUNTERED ME HAS LIVED TO TELL THE TALE—

OKAY. THAT'S INTERESTING.

BUT MY NAME'S NOT DANIEL, AND I HAVE NO IDEA WHAT YOU'RE TALKING ABOUT.

YOU HAVE A GOOD DAY.

bip

RING

WHAT WAS THAT?

WAS IT—

RRRRRING

RRRRRRING

I NORMALLY WOULDN'T HAVE COME TO SCHOOL... ...AFTER A DAY LIKE YESTER- DAY...

...BUT I CAN'T MISS A CHANCE TO SEE PHOEBE!

?!

WHAT'S WRONG?

WHAT'S GOING ON?

EXPLO-SIONS?

GET IN-SIDE!

MURMUR

MURMUR

BOOM

THIS CRAZINESS HAS TO STOP RIGHT NOW, BEFORE SOMEBODY GETS HURT.

MY CAR!

SHOOM

FWOOM

AIEEE!

WILLY!!

SLAM

I WAS SLEEPIN' IN, Y'KNOW?

I'M GETTING SHOT AT. THE SHELLS ARE ABOUT THE SIZE OF BOWLING BALLS.

WHOA!

WHAT'S GOING ON, DUDE?

COOL!

NOT COOL.

DANIEL

DAMN...CAN I
TURN IT BACK?
I GUESS I
SHOULD TRY.

THIS CUTIE?

YOU RULE, EMMA.

I OWE YOU ONE.

I OWE YOU.

THANKS FOR THINKING ME HERE. I JUST LOVE DOGGIES.

DANIEL? IS THAT YOU?

WHAT ARE YOU DOING HERE?

SORRY. IT WAS TOO LATE TO RING THE DOORBELL. I GOT INTO A MAJOR BLOWOUT WITH MY PARENTS...

I WOULDN'T STOP HELPING IF YOU TOLD ME TO.

WE'RE GOING TO FIND YOUR SISTER. SOMEHOW.

THANK YOU...

THAT'S THE POLICE FILE ON MY SISTER'S CASE. MY FOLKS DON'T KNOW I HAVE IT.

THERE HAD BEEN NO WITNESSES.

NO SIGN OF SUSPICIOUS VEHICLES. NO NOTHING.

ALLISON HAD GONE OUT TO PLAY AT AROUND ONE IN THE AFTERNOON.

WHEN HER MOTHER CHECKED ON HER, SHE WAS SIMPLY AND INEXPLICABLY GONE. AND SHE HAS NOT BEEN HEARD FROM AGAIN.

THIS HAS SOMETHING TO DO WITH SETH.

HERE'S A LIST TOO... HOW MANY KIDS DID HE KIDNAP?

!!

Potential Pattern

Awaiting GP

3907-4574

916-9543

3-5311

4355

LET'S TRY GOOGLING THE NAMES.

THE ONES HERE?

TAP

TAP

Malibu

IS SHE UP ALREADY?

NO SOUND OF A SHOWER.

WHERE IS SHE?

SHE'S NOT ANYWHERE IN THE BEDROOMS.

NOT IN THE ATTIC EITHER.

PHOEBE'S GONE.

DANIEL X

WHAT DO YOU MEAN SHE'S NOT IN THE HOUSE?

I NOTICED HER SCHOOL BAG'S GONE.

PHOEBE'S PARENTS!!

CHAPTER 4

MAYBE SHE WENT IN EARLY TO STUDY.

I'M SURE THERE'S A PERFECTLY REASONABLE EXPLANATION.

WHO ARE YOU CALLING?

THE POLICE.

HONEY, THERE'S NO NEED TO PANIC. WE SHOULD THINK THIS THROUGH.

SHE'S THE ONLY DAUGHTER WE HAVE LEFT.

YOU THINK IT THROUGH WHILE I DO SOMETHING.

THIS IS NOT GOOD.

PEOPLE JUST DON'T DISAPPEAR IN THE MIDDLE OF THE NIGHT.

AT LEAST NOT WILLINGLY.

PHOEBE!

IF PHOEBE WANTED TO HEAD TO MALIBU WITHOUT ME, SHE WOULD HAVE SAID SOMETHING. I WAS RIGHT THERE IN THE CLOSET, WASN'T I?

PHOEBE!!

SLAM

PHOEBE ISN'T HERE AT SCHOOL.

I DON'T WANT TO EVEN THINK ABOUT IT, BUT...

...DID SETH ALREADY...?

YOU'RE LIKE MY GUARDIAN ANGEL.

YEAH, OR MAYBE I'M THE ONE WHO LED SETH TO YOU.

PHOEBE!!

!

?!

WHAT?

!!

WHAT DO YOU THINK YOU'RE DOING?

AIEEEEEEEEE!!!!!

!!

THAT VOICE!!!

I'M COMING... HOLD ON!

PHOEBE!!

!

DANIEL!!

THUD

WHAM

SO THAT PART OF THE STORY WAS TRUE.

YOU REALLY ARE OFF-LOADING KIDS FROM THE EARTH. YOU'RE NOTHING BUT A SLAVE TRADER.

MOVE, MOVE, MOVE!

C'MON, THAT'S NOT ALL I AM.

DON'T FORGET ALL THE STEALING, MURDERING, AND DRUG DEALING I DO.

NOW THAT WE'VE COME FACE-TO-FACE, SETH...

...MY ONLY REGRET IS THAT YOU'RE NOT THE INSECTLIKE LOWLIFE WHO ACTUALLY KILLED MY FOLKS.

OH, I JUST MIGHT BE THEIR KILLER AFTER ALL.

NO, YOU'RE NOT. THE CREATURE WHO TOOK OUT MY PARENTS...

...THE ONE WHO IS GOING TO PAY WITH HIS LIFE...

...IS THE PRAYER.

YOU'RE ONLY *SIXTH* ON MY LIST, SETH. DREAM ON!

ARRGH!!

ACK!

THUD

RUMBLE

I NEED TO STAY UPBEAT... THE NIGHT IS DARKEST BEFORE THE DAWN.

I'M A LOSER, COMPLETE AND UTTER.

YEAH, RIGHT.

MAKES YOU STRONGER; CRIPPLES YOU FOREVER.

I GUESS IT WAS A FAMILY TRADITION.

YOU'RE NOT A LOSER!

EVERY CLOUD HAS A SILVER LINING.

YOU ARE NOT A LOSER, DANIEL.

WHAT DOESN'T KILL YOU MAKES YOU STRONGER.

OH, DANIEL.

YOU CAN'T DIE.

DON'T.

YOU CAN'T CRY, DANA.

MY HEART CAN STAND PRETTY MUCH ANYTHING EXCEPT SEEING YOU CRY.

BUT LOOK AT YOU.

I'VE NEVER SEEN YOU LIKE THIS. WHAT HAPPENED TO YOU?

BESIDES THAT...

...PHOEBE COOK FLIRTATION. WHAT WAS *THAT* ABOUT?

GOD, DANIEL.

SEEMS LIKE THE BLEEDING STOPPED.

HOW LONG HAS IT BEEN?

THE PAIN IS MANAGE-ABLE TOO.

AT LEAST I CAN SIT UP...

CLICK

HERE, BOY.

OH, WHAT'S WRONG?

DOES THE LITTLE DOGGIE HAVE A TUM-TUM ACHE?

DON'T WANT TO PLAY EPIC HERO ANYMORE?

HEY, HOW'S IT GOING?

DANIEL!

WE'RE TRYING TO FIND A LIFE-BOAT OR AN ESCAPE POD, BUT NO LUCK.

BUT YOU KNOW...

...EVEN IF WE FIND ONE, WE WON'T KNOW HOW TO OPER-ATE IT.

WE DON'T EVEN KNOW THE DIRECTION BACK TO EARTH.

THAT'S TRUE.

STILL, KEEP SEARCHING. IF NOT A WAY OUT, AT LEAST FIND A WAY TO STRIKE BACK AT SETH AND HIS GOONS.

OKAY, OKAY.

WAIT. LOOK AT THAT!

OH!

WHAT IS IT?

WILL LET YOU KNOW WHEN WE'RE SURE. TALK TO YOU LATER!

EMMA, DANA...

...WHAT ABOUT YOU GUYS?

HERE YOU GO!

IT'S A FRIENDSHIP BRACELET!

IT'LL KEEP YOU SAFE, OKAY?

HOW LONG HAVE YOU BEEN HERE?

MONTHS? YEARS?

DUNNO.

DUNNO.

WHERE ARE THE OLDER KIDS?

TAKEN AWAY.

YOU SMILED! YOU'RE MUCH CUTER WHEN YOU SMILE!

DANA...

WILLY, JOE, ANY UPDATES?

STILL NOT SURE.

I THINK IT MIGHT BE THE BRIDGE...

...BUT DON'T HOLD YOUR BREATH.

I'LL...

WHAT AM I THINKING?

THERE ISN'T GOING TO BE AN AGAIN.

...NEVER UNDERESTIMATE AN OPPONENT AGAIN.

I CALL.

WHAT THE—?!

THIS IS OUTRAGEOUS. I DON'T CARE IF YOU ARE DELIRIOUS.

THAT'S THE ACE OF CROSSES AND THE ACE OF CATS.

THOSE CARDS DON'T EXIST.

THOSE SUITS DON'T EVEN EXIST.

DANIEL, C'MON. THIS ISN'T LIKE YOU.

GEE, MOM.

I GUESS I HAVEN'T BEEN IN THE BEST OF MOODS SINCE SETH GAVE ME THIS NEW BELLY BUTTON HERE.

I'M ABOUT TO BE EXECUTED OR MAYBE SOMETHING WORSE...

...AND WHAT AM I DOING? SITTING HERE AND TAKING IT.

PORK CHOP, LISTEN TO ME! YOU THINK CHEATING AT CARDS IS A SHOCKER?

I KNOW SOMETHING THAT'LL BLOW YOUR MIND.

CLICK

GET HIM OUT.

WHERE TO NOW?

THE EXECUTION CHAMBER?

PUT HIS HOME UP ON THE BIG SCREEN.

WHY HAVE WE COME BACK?

AND WHY IS TERRA FIRMA GREENISH AT THE EDGES?

WHAT HAVE YOU DONE NOW, SETH?

ALPAR NOK?

MY HOME?

DANIEL X

TH-
THESE
RUINS...

CHAPTER 5

I'M SUCH A SHOW-OFF. LOVE TO RUB IT IN. I WANTED YOUR RACE TO SEE THAT THEIR DEFEAT WAS COMPLETE ACROSS THE UNIVERSE.

ALL HAIL THE RETURNING CONQUERED LOSER!

THAT'S *YOU*, BY THE WAY.

AFTER I'M DONE SHOWING YOU OFF...

...I'LL PUT YOU UP FOR AUCTION TO THE OTHER ALIENS.

MAYBE I'LL SELL YOU PIECE BY PIECE...

...AS EXPENSIVE ORNAMENTS.

YOUR FELLOW ALPARIANS?

THE FEW WHO ARE STILL ALIVE SCURRY THROUGH THE RUINS LIKE RATS.

WHERE IS EVERYONE?

!!

THEY HAVE NO POWERS, NO HOPE, NO REASON TO LIVE, REALLY.

BUT STILL THEY STUMBLE ON.

PATHETIC.

PROTECTORS OF THE UNIVERSE?

GUESS THEY SHOULD HAVE WORRIED MORE ABOUT PROTECTING THEMSELVES.

......

WHAT DO YOU MEAN, "PROTECTORS OF THE UNIVERSE"?

YOU ARE CLUELESS, AREN'T YOU?

BEHOLD, ALPAR NOK, THE HOME OF THE ALIEN HUNTERS...

...THE UNIVERSE'S ANSWER TO INJUSTICE AND EVIL!

YOUR PARENTS WERE SENT TO EARTH TO PROTECT THE OH-SO-SPECIAL HUMANS FROM THE OUTER ONES...

...AS THEY LIKE TO CALL US.

BECAUSE A FEW PATHETIC ALPARIANS WERE BORN WITH SOME ABILITY TO MANIPULATE THE UNIVERSAL FORCE...

...IT WAS THOUGHT YOU COULD PROTECT THE GOOD FROM THE EVIL.

AS IF GOOD AND EVIL AREN'T JUST FAIRY TALES MADE UP FOR SMALL CHILDREN.

THERE ARE THE *STRONG* AND THEN THERE ARE THE *WEAK.*

......

173

COULD IT BE THE AIR OF MY HOME-LAND?

I COULD SHATTER THESE SHACKLES EASILY, BUT THERE'S SO MANY OF THEM.

I NEED TO DO SOMETHING BEFORE SETH FINDS OUT THAT MY ABILITIES ARE COMING BACK.

SOMETHING OUTRAGEOUS TO DISTRACT THEM ALL.

EVER SINCE I STEPPED FOOT ON ALPAR NOK, POWER HAS BEEN FLOWING INTO ME.

...WAIT A SECOND.

THAT BUILDING IS LEANING TOWARD US.

DANIEL, IT DOES LOOK VERY UNSTABLE.

WE COULD DO THIS.

JUST A KICK WOULD MAKE IT—

TAP

CREAK

!!

CREAK

!!

HEY GUYS, NOT YET!

FIRE!!

IF I CAN JUST MAKE IT THERE!!

IT'S...THE ONLY GOOD THING LEFT IN THIS CRUMMY CITY, I GUESS.

IT'S... HARD TO DESCRIBE.

YOU HAVE TO SEE IT.

TAKE ME, TAKE ME!

TAKE ME!

OKAY.

ANYWAY, SHE WON'T STOP BUGGING ME UNTIL WE GO.

WHAT ARE YOU DOING?

CREAK

YOU'LL SEE.

TAKE ME!

TAKE ME!

WOW...

HEY, WAIT A SECOND, BEM.

THIS DOESN'T MAKE SENSE.

WHY WASN'T THIS DESTROYED LIKE EVERYTHING ELSE?

THE SKY ISN'T REAL. IT'S A DOME.

MY DAD TOLD ME IT'S MADE OF A SPECIAL GLASS THAT DOES SOMETHING TO LIGHT, LETS IT IN BUT NOT OUT.

LONG AGO, THERE WAS A WAR AND THE CHILDREN'S PARK WAS BOMBED, SO THEY MADE THIS NEW ONE INDOORS.

EVEN THE OUTER ONES COULDN'T FIND IT.

THANK GOD...

ALL IS NOT LOST.

RUSTLE

ELEPHANTS!!

HOW DO YOU DO?

MY NAME IS CHORDATA.

!!!

TELEPATHY—?!

?

MY NAME IS...

DANIEL.

YES, I REMEMBER YOU FROM WHEN YOU WERE A BABY.

YOU USED TO COME HERE EVERY DAY WITH YOUR MOTHER. WE WOULD COMMUNICATE LIKE THIS.

HEY GUYS, COULD YOU EXPLAI—

DASH

THERE WAS A RUMOR THAT AN ALIEN PERSON ESCAPED FROM ERGENT SETH'S STARSHIP.

HE SENT YOU, DIDN'T HE?

NOW HE'S SENDING SPIES, IS THAT IT?

I'M NOT A SPY.

LIKE YOU WOULDN'T LIE TO ME IF YOU WERE.

SLAP

HER HAND NEVER MOVED—SHE SMACKED ME WITH HER MIND!

LET GO OF ME AND—

THANK YOU.

YOU'VE HELPED ME REMEMBER...

...THE WAY IT USED TO BE.

FINALLY...

...I HAVE A REAL CONNECTION TO MY FAMILY.

TO WHO I AM.

TO WHAT I WAS PUT IN THE UNIVERSE TO DO.

!!

!!

THUD

DANIEL?!

WHAT'S WRONG?

URGH...

...THE PAIN...

WHAT HAPPENED TO YOU?

YOUR STOMACH?

TELL ME, BEFORE YOU PASS OUT.

I WAS... SHOT...

...WITH...A 24/24 OPUS MAGNUM.

MUST HAVE USED A DELAYED FRAG ROUND.

TINY CHARGE INSIDE THE BULLET. CAN BE ACTIVATED AT A LATER DATE. EVEN BY REMOTE CONTROL.

DANIEL X

BOOM

...EXPLO-
SION?

WHERE AM
I....? AH,
SURGERY...

CHAPTER 6

A
SCREW-
DRIVER?
COME
ON!

WELL,
WHAT
DO YOU
KNOW?

I CAN'T
BELIEVE
IT.

YOU'RE
ACTUALLY
ALIVE.

WHAT HAP-PENED?

THE SMOKE?

I MANAGED TO GET THE BULLET OUT OF YOU, BUT IT BLEW UP...

...RIGHT WHEN I WAS TRYING TO TOSS IT OUT THE WINDOW.

HOW ARE YOU FEELING?

WELL...

...LIKE A MILLION BUCKS.

THANK YOU, UM...

I DIDN'T CATCH YOUR NAME, DOCTOR.

NO DOCTOR. JUST BLALEEN.

THANK YOU, EH, BLA-LEEN, FOR SAVING MY LIFE.

FOR... WHATEVER YOU DID HERE.

WAIT A SECOND.

YOU HAVEN'T SEEN MY WATCH, HAVE YOU?

I WAS WEARING IT A...

AH, DON'T MENTION IT.

OH, DEAR ME.

NO.

PLEASE, NO.

204

OF COURSE NOT.

JUST A LITTLE SURGEON HUMOR.

BUT ENOUGH JOKING AROUND, DANIEL.

YOU NEED REST.

YOU ALMOST DIED ON THE OPERATING TABLE.

YOU RECOGNIZED ME BEFORE, DIDN'T YOU?

WHAT DO YOU KNOW ABOUT ME?

I KNOW MANY THINGS.

I KNOW YOU WERE GIVEN A HUMAN NAME, BECAUSE YOU AND YOUR PARENTS WERE HEADING TO EARTH.

......

A DEAR FRIEND.

DOWN THE HATCH NOW, DANIEL.

GRAFF WINS ALL-CITY!

GRAFF? MY FATHER? MY FATHER AS A YOUNG MAN?

WHY WOULD THE OLD WOMAN HAVE A PICTURE OF MY—

BLALEEN, WHO ARE YOU, REALLY?

DANIEL!

LITTLE
ONES...

...SAY
HELLO
TO YOUR
GREAT-
COUSIN
DANIEL.

DANIEL X,
TO BE
PRECISE.

HE DOESN'T
USE A FAMILY
NAME BECAUSE
HE DOESN'T
HAVE A FAMILY.

UNTIL NOW,
THAT IS.

I'M YOUR COUSIN LYLAH.

I'M YOUR UNCLE KRAFFLEPROG, YOUR MOM'S BROTHER.

TELL ME EVERY-THING.

WHO I AM.

WHO THE ALIEN HUNTERS ARE.

WHAT MY PARENTS WERE DOING ON EARTH.

WHERE—

WHOA, WHOA!

I'LL GIVE YOU THE SHORT VERSION, DANIEL.

LISTEN NOW.

MANY HUNDREDS OF YEARS AGO, OUR SPACE PROBES DISCOVERED EARTH.

WHAT AMAZED US WAS HOW SIMILAR OUR PLANETS WERE, IN TEMPERATURE, ATMOSPHERE, BODIES OF WATER.

IT WAS DISCOVERED THAT THE HUMAN HEART WAS ALSO SIMILAR TO THAT OF ALPARIANS, PHYSICALLY, AND IN OTHER WAYS AS WELL. IT WAS SUGGESTED THAT OUR RACES MIGHT HAVE DESCENDED FROM A SINGLE ANCESTOR.

UNFORTUNATELY, WE SOON LEARNED THE OUTER ONES HAD ALREADY DISCOVERED EARTH AND WERE WORKING TO COLONIZE AND TAKE IT OVER.

MY SON, GRAFF, MET AND FELL IN LOVE WITH YOUR MOTHER, ATRELDA, WHEN THEY WERE AT UNIVERSITY.

THEY BOTH HAD POWERS, DANIEL, TELEPATHY AND TRANSFORMING ABILITY.

THEY COULD, WELL, CREATE THINGS AT WILL.

IT'S RARE, BUT IT HAPPENS HERE.

DID YOU TELL HIM ABOUT HIS RATING?

THIS IS LIKE A MEMORY HOME MOVIE.

IT'S ONE OF OUR ABILITIES.

!!

THAT'S—!

WILLY!

EMMA!

DANA!

JOE!

WAIT A SECOND!

YES, THEY WERE YOUR FRIENDS FROM PRE-SCHOOL.

MY, HOW YOU USED TO GET ON.

BUT WHERE ARE THEY NOW? I HAVE TO SEE THEM IMMEDIATELY.

THAT'S JOE, WILLY, EMMA, AND DANA. MY FRIENDS!

YOU FORMED A FRIENDSHIP BOND, CALLED A DRANG...

...THAT IS RARELY SEEN AMONG OUR PEOPLE. VERY POWERFUL, DANIEL. VERY SPECIAL.

THEIR BODIES WERE NEVER RECOVERED.

THEY'RE PRESUMED DEAD, DANIEL.

SETH...

I'M COMING FOR YOU.
I SWEAR I AM.

I KNOW
THINGS
LOOK
BAD NOW,
DANIEL.

CRASH

WHAT THE—?!

PREPARE TO FIRE ON MY ORDER!

AND SUM-MON MORE BACKUP.

I WANT A FULL SQUADRON OF BATTLE TANKS AND MISSILE DRONES!

GET ME A MILLION SQUAD-RONS!

ANYBODY MOVES...

...THEY'RE DEAD.

SAME GOES FOR YOU, SETH.

ON EARTH, THIS IS WHAT THEY CALL A MEXICAN STANDOFF.

YOU MOVE, YOU DIE.

I MOVE, I DIE.

I'LL TEACH YOU A LESSON.

IT WON'T TAKE LONG.

DANIEL!!

YOU DID IT!!

YOU THERE.

M-ME?

YES, YOU.

WHAT'S YOUR NAME?

K...KROTH-GARK, SIR.

KROTH-GARK.

I HAVEN'T DECIDED IF I'M GOING TO LET YOU LIVE OR NOT.

WOULD YOU LIKE TO INFLUENCE MY DECISION?

YES, VERY MUCH.

THEN DO YOURSELF A BIG FAVOR AND LET THE KIDS FROM EARTH GO. ALL OF THEM.

YOU GOT IT, SIR.

RIGHT AWAY, RIGHT AWAY. YOU HEARD THE MAN!

......

UM... THANK YOU... AND...

...I FOUND THIS ON THE SHIP. I THOUGHT IT MIGHT BE IMPORTANT.

MY LAPTOP! THANK YOU!

SO...

...WHY ARE WE...

...BACK ON EARTH AGAIN?!

IF WE'D STAYED ON ALPAR NOK...

...WE WOULD HAVE HAD A FEAST EVERY DAY!

......

I LOVE IT HERE.

IT'S A GREAT, GREAT PLANET.

x

242

THIS IS MY HOME.

BESIDES, I HAVE TO FINISH THE WORK MY PARENTS STARTED.

I CAN'T EVEN IMAGINE HOW I WOULD FEEL...

...IF SOMETHING HAPPENED TO EARTH WHILE I WAS GONE.

I'LL MISS MY GRAND-MA...

...BUT I'LL GET TO SEE HER AGAIN, I'M SURE.

DANIEL...

...NO MATTER WHAT YOU DECIDE TO DO...

...REMEM-BER THAT YOU'VE ALWAYS GOT US!

BE AFRAID, ALIENS!

BE VERY, VERY AFRAID!

TO BE CONTINUED IN DANIEL X, VOL. 2!

MAXIMUM
RIDE
CHAPTER 1

YAWN~

WHEN WE FIRST MOVED INTO THIS SECLUDED HOUSE...

...JEB BATCHELDER TOOK CARE OF US, LIKE A DAD.

GOOD MORNING, JEB.

TWO YEARS AGO, HE DISAPPEARED. WE ALL KNEW HE WAS DEAD, BUT WE DIDN'T TALK ABOUT IT.

AND NOW, AS THE OLDEST, I'M TRYING TO KEEP THINGS RUNNING IN HIS PLACE...AS BEST I CAN!

WHUMP!!

ACK!

WOBBLE

WOBBLE

I'LL POUR JUICE.

WHO MOVED THE TABLE NEXT TO THE STAIRS?!

SORRY, IGGY.

THE STAIRCASE JUST LOOKED SO EMPTY.

DON'T FORGET I'M BLIND.

THEN PLEASE ACT LIKE YOU ARE.

FLOP

RUMMAGE RUMMAGE

UMM... WISH THE FOOD FAIRIES HAD COME...

FANG!! WILL YOU QUIT THAT?!

QUIT WHAT? BREATHING?

MAKE SOME NOISE WHEN YOU MOVE! YOU STARTLED ME!

I'LL MAKE EGGS.

WOBBLE

I DON'T WANT MAX TO BURN OUR LAST FRYING PAN.

......

Huh? Fang, when did you get up??

FINE. I'LL GO GET NUDGE AND ANGEL.

......

Look for MAXIMUM RIDE: THE MANGA in bookstores now!

GET YOUR MANGA FIX!!

Can't wait for the next volume of the *DANIEL X* or *MAXIMUM RIDE* manga to hit the bookstores? Now you can read the latest installments of your favorite manga in *YEN PLUS*, the monthly online magazine!

Just go to **www.yenpress.com** and hit the magazine tab to sign up for a monthly subscription, and you can read new chapters of *MAXIMUM RIDE*, *DANIEL X*, and more before adding the books to your collection!

Reading great manga online has never been easier!

3/16

DANIEL X: THE MANGA ①

JAMES PATTERSON
WITH MICHAEL LEDWIDGE
& SEUNGHUI KYE

Adaptation and Illustration: SeungHui Kye

Lettering: JuYoun Lee & Abigail Blackman

DANIEL X, THE MANGA, Vol. 1 © 2010 by James Patterson

Illustrations © 2010 Hachette Book Group, Inc.

Yen Press
Hachette Book Group
1290 Avenue of the Americas, New York, NY 10104

www.HachetteBookGroup.com
www.YenPress.com

Yen Press is an imprint of Hachette Book Group, Inc. The Yen Press name and logo are trademarks of Hachette Book Group, Inc.

First Yen Press Edition: October 2010

ISBN: 978-0-316-07764-4

10 9 8 7 6 5

BVG

Printed in the United States of America